ALSO BY KEVIN YOUNG

POETRY
Brown
Blue Laws: Selected & Uncollected Poems 1995–2015
Book of Hours
Ardency
Dear Darkness
For the Confederate Dead
To Repel Ghosts: the remix
Black Maria
Jelly Roll: a blues
To Repel Ghosts
Most Way Home

NONFICTION
Bunk: The Rise of Hoaxes, Humbug, Plagiarists, Phonies, Post-Facts, and Fake News
The Grey Album: On the Blackness of Blackness

AS EDITOR
African American Poetry: 250 Years of Struggle & Song
The Hungry Ear: Poems of Food & Drink
The Collected Poems of Lucille Clifton 1965–2010 (with Michael S. Glaser)
Best American Poetry 2011
The Art of Losing: Poems of Grief & Healing
Jazz Poems
John Berryman: Selected Poems
Blues Poems
Giant Steps: The New Generation of African American Writers

STONES

STONES

Poems

KEVIN YOUNG

ALFRED A. KNOPF, NEW YORK, 2024

THIS IS A BORZOI BOOK
PUBLISHED BY ALFRED A. KNOPF

Copyright © 2021 by Kevin Young

All rights reserved. Published in the United States by Alfred A. Knopf,
a division of Penguin Random House LLC, New York, and distributed in
Canada by Penguin Random House Canada Limited, Toronto.

www.aaknopf.com

Knopf, Borzoi Books, and the colophon are registered trademarks of
Penguin Random House LLC.

The lost toys and objects that appear on the cover of this book were
all found and photographed by Tracey Williams, a beachcomber in
Cornwall, England.

Library of Congress Cataloging-in-Publication Data
Names: Young, Kevin, [date] author.
Title: Stones : poems / Kevin Young.
Description: New York : Alfred A. Knopf, 2021. |
Identifiers: LCCN 2020057384 (print) | LCCN 2020057385 (ebook) |
    ISBN 9781524732561 (hardcover) | ISBN 9781524732578 (ebook) |
    ISBN 9781524711153 (trade pbk.)
Subjects: LCGFT: Poetry.
Classification: LCC PS3575.O798 S86 2021 (print) |
    LCC PS3575.O798 (ebook) | DDC 811/.54—dc23
LC record available at https://lccn.loc.gov/2020057384
LC ebook record available at https://lccn.loc.gov/2020057385

Cover photograph by Tracey Williams
Cover design by Kelly Blair

Manufactured in the United States of America
Published September 28, 2021
1st Printing

for Mack

The stones hope
to remember

Contents

RED RIVER

TRUMPET

STONES

Resume

Where the train once rained
        through town
like a river, where the water

rose in early summer
        & froze come winter—
where the moon

of the outhouse shone
        its crescent welcome,
where the heavens opened

& the sun wouldn't quit—
        past the gully or gulch
or holler or ditch

I was born.
        Or, torn—
Dragged myself

atop this mountain
        fueled by flour, butter-
milk, grease fires.

Where I'm from
        women speak
in burnt tongues

& someone's daddy dug
        a latrine so deep
up from the dark

dank bottom springs a tree.

OBLIVION

*It'll look
like you are lost—
just keep going*

Halter

Nothing can make, make me want
      to stay
in this world—

not the grass
      with its head of hair
turning grey—

not the sway-back horse
      in the field
I swear I almost saw

start to saunter—

nor the bent shadows
      late in the day
drawing close—

the neighbor's boat
      not yet docked
gathering snow—

not the dream
      with the moose hunched
in its crown

shedding velvet
      led by a silver halter
through the shaded campground

a shawl over its shoulders
      like a caftan on a grandmother
or her rocker

whenever she's no longer there.

Not the brass nail-heads
      on the Adirondack chair
I put together, sweating,

this morning, that creaks
      but still
does hold—

nor the cries of the others
      above water, beloved
bright voices of summer

echoing like the ice cream man
      in his whirring truck—
along the curb his lights flash

like an ambulance
      playing the tune
you cannot name—yet know—

except this babbling, like a light
      barely shining,
from below the baby's cracked door.

Dolor

Start here. With the dolor
      that is early September
bringing new weather—

the sky a cold color
      coming on, my son
one year older

& able, among the letters,
      to find his name.
I know I am not alone, even

if it is my home—
      above us, like crows,
circle clouds we seek

to keep. We sleep long,
      if not sound—
our feet finding morning.

Till the end
      we sing
into the wind.

Spruce

Sing a song of going under—
        the elms, or my father.
In the back corner

of the yard the spruce splinters
        under snow, half
of it gone. The fall is all.

Grief's evergreen.
        Even plastic
can get sick. That's not the half of it—

one day, healthy, under
        the white weight,
the deep, the maple snapped & took

some of the house with it.
        Whenever I am outside,
says my toddler, *I'm always*

a goner. His words
        a stone on my tongue—
sung above

the snow & thunder.
        The thank of apple.
The thirst

of acorn. The spruce
        bowed down
to the snowed

ground. Today sun will
            send us south,
we pray, our arms around

the trunk of what
            we've lost.
Fill my hands

with splinters, sir,
            stuff my mouth
with ice—

say yes.

Hum

I am learning how to sleep
       again, to love
the descent, or is it,

lying here, a rising up
       to summit
where sleep wanders

till waking. And when
       I cannot, when the water
leaches into everything

& capsizes me, I wonder
       where you are,
father, if anywhere

at all—
       Does sleep
know you? Does day? Such nights,

dreams fill my waking
       & worry weathers
the dark, the light horribly

leaking through the curtains—
       or, awake,
early, I wait for it to seep in

from the east. *The land*
       of dead in the west.
The hum of sun—

none, none, then suddenly
        up—it too
cannot be sated

or slaked off, brother sun,
        mother moon,
father you cannot find

though somewhere still shines.

Egrets

Some say beauty
         may be the egret
in the field

who follows after
         the cows
sensing slaughter—

but I believe
         the soul is neither
air nor water, not

this winged thing
         nor the cattle
who moan

to make themselves
         known.
Instead, the horses

standing almost fifteen
         hands high—
like regret they come

most the time
         when called.
Hungry, the greys eat

from your palm,
         tender-toothed—
their surprising

plum-dark tongues
        flashing quick
& rough as a match—

striking your hand,
        your arm, startled
into flame.

Ivy

The throats of the trees
      choked by ivy
still sing

with birds, hidden,
      who bide
their time, midnight

sending them silent.
      The chickens who once
woke me early

have strayed far
      from this yard
into a sky they

& I
      only dreamt of—
the stove calls us

like the quiet
      of this place, the graves
awaiting names.

Clearing

It's a strange place
       to try & find
God—inside

a building. Better off
       in a field whose owner,
if any, has let the ivy

overtake it, shotgun shacks
       pulled down, abandoned
beneath the green

that has no borders
       & thus is beautiful.
Once seen, you won't

later, in shadow, be able
       to hunt it down—
that meadow we sat

awhile, unbit,
       shadeless, then went
on without.

Oblivion

In the field the cows consider
        oblivion, mulling
it over. They & their many

        stomachs know nothing
stays lost forever—that grass, almost
        cruel, resurrects again,

again. They know even
        drought will end
though the family they belong to

        forgets. Cows know the slow
closing eye of the pond
        will once more open

& the sky—rain will find
        their bowed backs,
the burnt earth's offering.

        Cows keep no cry, only
a slave's low moan.
        This slight rise

they must climb.

PRAISE WINE

Anything
can be saved.
Or praised—

Sanctuary

Sent into an oblivion
      of their own
making, the women of the Amen

Corner raise hands,
      holler, while up
the aisle wanders

a soul once lost—
      now the tongues
have taken him,

Amen, away
      from us, yet among—
Amen—think of the heart

alone with what
      cannot be sung,
or undone—

here, we don't dare.
      Anything can
be found. Redeemed

by the reedy voice
      of the choir director,
his hands egging

everyone on, their voices
      & our own. The soloist
stretches forth, unsure

at first, her voice
        cracks on its climb
to the rafters. Anything

can be saved.
        Or praised—
this sanctuary where happy

isn't what happens
        but may be
found, gotten, held,

almost hoarded.
        The stained
glass patched.

The red road
        to the altar worn
& well.

High Water

What does
      the water want?
Enters where

it is not
      welcome, jacks
up the foundation

uneven
      & splits the wood
like a look—

it rusts
      it rusts
rusts the roof through—

drops by unannounced
      when your house a mess,
rifles through Mama's

drawers, papers, borrows
      books for weeks
& returns them

waterlogged, dogged,
      without no note—
or knock—plucks

baby pictures
      out their frames
& blurs

all the names—
        endless,
oblivious,

it apologizes
        & blesses
& barely says sorry—

in a word
        you could
call it *family*.

Kith

All week I have wondered
        what *kith*
meant—

always paired
        with *kin,* can it be
the same thing?

Kin seems like
        like, like *kind,*
as in our kind,

us—kindness,
        we hope,
or something to like.

Kith is more
        helpless, married
as it is to kin—

Kith is what you find
        in the cemetery, names
effaced from their graves,

names you may not
        know, but share,
or share though don't yet know.

Kith is not
        yesterday—
that's ancestry—nor

is it today—*kin*
      keeps that close—
no, kith

is tomorrow
      & who knows?
Is outliving

the dead, but means
      the dead too, resting
here on the sill

among the blue
      bottles—both the flies
& the glass

that once held what?
      Kith
is that. The pair

of shoes that still
      keep the wearer's shape
after removed—

whether moments ago, dog-tired,
      or years later,
still standing—

though nobody asked
      them to—long beyond
when the wearer's gone.

Praise Dance

For Mama
  Annie, his great
grandmother, at her 85th birthday

& at her feet, my second cousin
   performs a praise
dance, whirling, bobbing—

pale gloves
   a magician's, his face
painted white

like a tribesman,
   mine.
Nothing

disappears. Only
   this bowing—
thanking her

& how all we got here.

Tongues

During his benediction
       prayer—before Mama
Annie dances

to Stevie Wonder, in the dress
       my mother bought her—*Happy
Birthday to Ya*—

her wave praise
       applauding her own
existence,

my uncle the preacher
       asks us: *If you die tonight
do you know*

where you're going? Folks raise
       & join hands, lower
heads, & my son

won't sit still
       for anyone—even God
whose tongues the waiter

turns fluent in.
       Mama Annie's fever
for the Lord—Uncle Sunnyman

the preacher's hands
       on her forehead
healing, or telling

her temperature, the way
        Mama Annie once must've
with him. After hellfire

comes the music
        of mortality—the plaid,
three-piece bishop leaves

so we can drink.
        I'm not
an alcoholic, says my cousin,

but an akaholik—*I only drink*
        Hennessey.
Later, to the tune

of *Superman, ho!*
        my son, drunk
with motion & dizzy

with family, spins
        like a world, falling
out on the buckling

banquet floor.

Fifth Sunday

In my childhood
      mind, there were miles
between Mama Annie's

house & her house
      of worship we spent
hours in

come Sunday—
      instead, older now, see
it's only a stone's throw.

Across from church
      the leaning tombs
of her folks, sister,

more. Maybe
      it wasn't the pastor
but this past buried

just beyond the stained
      glass, chased
her from that door?

Now she worships
      even nearer, at a temple
thrown together right

behind her house.
      My son leaping
like a year

between the stones.

BONEYARD

They took everything
from her—
except breath

Sting

Burying weather—
      the stark heat
we sweat in, saying

our goodbyes. Flowers
      bend in it,
embarrassed

almost—the agony
      of growing, this great
effort, trying

not to die—our eulogy
      the daisies write
by sunlight, in storm,

in the fall of what
      greets us all. Hurt
is not meant

by the blades of summer
      the bumblebee somehow
swims around—

then away. For now,
      the sting
of being—

tomorrow already
      a memory, a bite
bright & burning.

Body Shop

My great-grandfather rests
      almost to the fence
of the body shop

we first stopped at
      to ask
directions home.

My son picking up small stones
      as if he knows
where we're going—

Along the road
      this chimney is all
that's left

of a house long since
      burnt down—
battered brick—

reddened finger
      in a rain-fed field
aimed above.

Dog Tags

Of us there is
         always less.
The days hammer

past, artificial daisies
         at the grave.
Words I didn't choose

for my father's headstone
         & those that came instead
to live around my neck,

dog tags a tin
         pendulum on my chest.
On my mother's side,

my cousin, too young,
         dirt a pile above her
but no stone, nothing

but the tinfoil name
         from the funeral home—
the fresh plastic

flowers that still wilt
         in this heat.
At blackjack

she lost
         everything my great-
aunt & -uncle had saved,

even their low ranch
   where I first
knew blue glass, plastic

covering the rug
   & the good couch
in the sitting room

no one dared sit.
   The prickly underside
of the clear runner a cactus

you couldn't help
   but touch. Uncle Wilmer's
pickup long paid off

now stares empty
   under somebody
else's tree. The liars

& book-cookers
   came with their knives
offering her

seconds, & she
   sat & ate—
once you've tasted

the stone-filled fruit
   of the underworld
you may never return.

They took everything
   from her
my mother says, both

of us shaking
        our heads, disbelieving
how exacting

death is, how deep
        the shade—
except breath.

She was in debt
        & dead within
a year, went through money

like water—
        And that didn't
last long either.

Fog

Despite the heat
          it is forever
winter here—

mounds we must
          step past,
all night the steady

piling & much
          the next day.
Bright but you can

barely see—
          the fog that finds
my glasses

whenever I exit
          the car left
idling like the dead

among tilted stones.
          It is snow
to see you

buried here—a frozen
          fallen light
we lie down & try

making angels in.

Vault

The earth will eat you alive—
        fire ants at
my love's feet, biting,

send her seeking shade.
        There's no high
ground here, only the dead

in their vaults, half under
        & half above
like us. My toddler son skips stone

to stone, hollering happily
        on the slabs with bodies
unmarked beneath.

Some we know, or guess
        by their neighbors
planted in the red dirt with no plaque

or stone. Words worn
        by weather, burning
away a date

or a name, leaving only
        a carved finger
pointing above.

Look down, remember—
        or you'll find yourself
knee deep among the mounds

of ants who mourn
        like we do, a host
of red devouring you.

Tomorrow our bug bites
        will bloom—
little memorials, funeral

pyres, burial
        barrows risen
in our skin

red as the earth. Each
        a place something
came & went

without our knowing—
        like these names
on old graves

scratched by hand
        in stone. Tomorrow
we'll itch for all we feel

can't yet see.

Boneyard

Like heat he seeks them,
      my son, thirsting
to learn those

he don't know
      are his dead—
some with his name

carved in the stones
      he leaps on
& between. Their fake

flowers will outlive
      even doubt.
Beside the boneyard

six men nail & saw
      together a house,
their lumber

sliced even, still
      golden. They build
a kind of heaven,

chipping in—something
      all yours, the neighbors
honking hello

as they roll by,
      no rush, envious—
wondering under

their breath how long
will paradise take
& whether you'll finish

in this lifetime.

BOUQUET

GONE BUT NOT
FORGOTTON

Reprieve

On reprieve
      from the rain
but not the heat—

we watch it
      gather like flowers
or the men who build

a house in fits
      & starts
across the street.

They saw
      & nail what
I can't see—a coffin

cut to measure,
      or a wedding dress
sewn closed

along the pinked seams.
      The earth
stitched shut

above the heads
      of the dead—
whose hands, before

buried, held flowers
      or rosaries
or only each other.

The dirt will try
      to forget.
The stones hope

to remember.
      The grass sings
its praises depending on

the weather.

Swallows

The sun swallows
     our shadows.
It makes

& shrinks them, some
     still cling
to the trees—

noon removes
     all stains of shade
while we wander

among stones, pilgrims
     seeking the past,
bowing at the crosses

carved into old markers
     by hand.
At the gravecutter's shop

a black cat tiptoes
     among the granite
carved with saxophones

& basketballs for the teen
     gone too soon—
RIP for someone long under

whose family never could pay.
     Gravestones too
can have a resting place

they get lost in.
        Mostly they make
their way here

& there, throw
        lone shadows
across these slabs

of concrete the dead
        sleep beneath.
Others remain

ghost ships adrift,
        at sea,
awaiting names—

silhouettes
        cast upon water
their only banner.

Chisel

Our words hope to mend
        what wind
wants instead—

carved by hand, this stone
        soft enough to chisel
& scalpel in

a finger aimed
        at heaven. REST
WE WILL MEET AGAIN.

FATHER
        & HOPE carved
curved above a lamb

asleep, kneeling.

Lilies

Almost June
       yet the blooms
are already done

here among
       my grandfather
& foremothers & my father

planted too early—
       WE MISS
YOU BROTHER.

He will not see
       another May,
whose colors fiery

surround us
       & now him—will not
know his grandson

& namesake, ever since
       cruel April
stole him. Father,

never will you know

how words blossom
       from my son
this Memorial Day, visiting

your stone—
       hot, up, more,
more, he sings—

The lilies
       we leave
will tip over in wind

near your name
       my son doesn't yet know
though it's his own.

Bouquet

Tell the sky—
        quit stealing
you away.

Above, storm clouds
        only threaten
& will not stay.

The sun finds us
        like fear, or family,
fills the stomach

& asks to borrow
        you awhile. Like sugar forgets
to bring you back.

My skin
        an orange peeling.
There aren't

enough words—
        only these, halting, half
erased in stone—

MY WIFE IS RESTING
        WITH JESUS. But just
how long the widower

sat here, staring at the hole
        no dirt can fill, the wound
in the ground above

his twenty-year-old bride
whose stone now tilts
& wilts like a bouquet

I cannot say.

Exposure

Later I will leave
      or lose
the camera I brought

to capture all
      I saw with—
to record my dead

in photos so later
      I could carve names
& dates into the tree

called family.
      Lost
from a pocket, felled

or stolen——who was it later found
      those graves
my camera caught? My son

among stones, the heat—
      mounds of earth
& plastic bouquets in a corner

piled like a mass grave,
      needed no longer.
GONE BUT NOT

FORGOTTON.
      Who kept all I saw
as their own? Watcher

but not witness—a witness must
　　　　not only see
but later say. I picture

whoever found the shots
　　　　erasing frame
after frame, exposed steady

& slow as the words
　　　　one day even the stone
lets go.

ROSE ROOM

I'm done being
in love with
what leaves—

Blackout

In the bar the drunks are
        tender as mourners—
talking low, rubbing

each other's backs
        like a grave—
gathered here to grieve

what all they've managed to leave.

This hour at least
        the beer is happy
& nearly free.

Wednesday well
        drinks half off—
these are sorrow's

regulars, where once,
        electricity out
Up South, I headed

to find the cause,
        beer warming slow
in the tap, not just

the hand. Rumors
        of explosions,
of smoke from a manhole

swirled. Two dead.
        Turns out it wasn't
that at all—only the heat wave

washing ashore. The bar's bell
       still tolls, tip jar full
of soggy bills the barkeep

undertakes
       to count later, slowly,
knowing what can't

be held. Still alive
       like the wine,
we can't help

but try.

Brown Water

Like anger, the water
      here comes bottled
or boils over—flows

from taps rusty
      as remembrance.
We buy ice

in bulk, & pork, stowaway
      the wood we make
a fire from—

hickory, pecan,
      a little bit
of peach for taste—

my cousin the preacher's first
      to fix him
a plate. After, our bones

tossed to the dogs, he'll show
      us dirty pictures
on his phone

of his many *wives*, he calls them,
      each one we toast to—
our plastic cups spilling Courvoisier

or Remy. Laughing we go
      to the refreshment sto'
to buy some more

of that brown water.
        I'm a Baptist
he says, *but I have*

Catholic inclinations.
        Ours
is an anthem waiting

to be written.

House Rules

CHARCOAL

      & ROSE ROOM LOUNGE

House Rules:

Proper Dress
      Picture ID
Required

Age 25 yrs or Older
      No Muscle Shirts
T-Shirts No Service

No excuse

Tonsure

Forever you find
       your father
in other faces—

a balding head
       or beard enough
to send you following

for blocks after
       to make sure
you're wrong, or buying

some stranger a beer
       to share. Well, not
just one—and here,

among a world that mends
       only the large things,
let the shadow grow

upon your face
       till you feel
at home. It's all

yours, this father
       you make
each day, the one

you became when yours
       got yanked away.
Take your place between

the men bowed
      at the bar, the beer
warming, glowing faint

as a heart—lit
      from within & just
a hint bitter.

Soldiers

When we're low
  we roll
to the corner, near-empties

in our hands.
  Made of stones
the road rough

behind our tires
  spits & kicks.
When we reach the store

you can buy
  anything here,
so long as it's Bud

or Light.
  As long as someone
else pays.

Do you got change—

On the counter lengths
  of boudin curl
like a cat

or a hog's tail—
  the woman will cut
you a link like fate

& you got yourself
  a meal.
Home again, still

cold, tomorrow's soldiers
shall become targets
peppered with pellets.

Sandy Road

The roads here
        only lately got names.
Before, we lived

on Rural Route
        blank, the mailbox
far enough away

across a field
        it was worth a trek
only once a week

to find what the world had
        to say. Its metal mouth
a garfish few found.

No streets, just this
        rushing stream
after a hard rain. Today

the roads remain
        mostly ditchwater & dirt—
small stones that migrate

but never far. Today
        my auntie complains
the roads were named

for grandnieces born yesterday
        who didn't do nothin—
instead of after great-

grandfathers & others
      who cut their way
back here by hand

& hatchet, wheelbarrow
      & know-how,
trucking even

daylight in. These
      are our saints—
our *Emiles* & *Ad-oms*

& *Bananes* who made
      these roads right
as rain. We still live

in their straightaways
      & curves, slowly
buying back

what so & so's foolishness
      fretted away. Once the whole
doggone world was young—

once there were no words
      for things
& people had to wait

among the green
      & listen first,
making sure

the things themselves,
      the very stones,
would tell you what

they wished to be named.

Joy

Once we bathed
      in Joy.
Ivory, once.

Mister
      Bubbles, if lucky.
Sometimes accidentally

our own pee.
      Mostly us little ones
got soaked

& scrubbed like dishes, teeth
      chipped like our tub.
We filled it up.

This was back when dirt
      & each other
was all we loved,

my cousins & I.
      How we hated
getting clean—it wasn't

so much the water
      or the cold after
as it was all that change—

the grey circling the drain.

Evenings we bathed
in Palmolive green.
Other nights,

Dawn.

Cockcrow

Long before dawn
        the roosters begin
what only a fool

would call a song—
        their wailing
wakes us, a call

not to arms (though the sound
        makes one
want to get a gun)

but for legs & eyes
        to start,
for logs to find

their way into fire—
        or a fan to send
what breeze there is

about. This house
        built on stilts
does not stir

so much as shake
        now that my son's
thrown awake—he runs

his mother & himself
        ragged. The rooster's
yawning yell

tells the day
hurry up—
dividing what is
from what shall be.

Russet

I want to drink
        the day down.
Maybe next

the night—first,
        we'll find
our feet, our feet

the floor. The blue beyond
        the window
returns like a mother

after work, collapsing into
        the living room.
I'm home. I'm done being

in love with
        what leaves—
autumn gathers

in the trees, russet,
        then tries
not to fall asleep

on the cold ground.
        God, it is
hard being happy

if you try—
        instead, be like
this slow

yellow. Let go.

RED RIVER

*What balm
the weather offers*

Skeleton Key

Conductor of the Quiet—
      Keeper
of the Lost—

Singer of all
      the songs
longing I have forgot—

Lead me from this
      yard of bones
these houses of stone

to the wooden home
      where my mother
got herself born—

later torn down
      & turned to fire—
I remember well

the ground that shone
      four feet below
through its raised, holey floor.

Lead me over
      the Red River
past the plantations

my uncles picked cotton in—
      & sometimes my mother—
Shepherd me

past fields
        filled with storm
& still-short corn

Let me be reborn
        among the overgrowth
& the shotgun houses

giving up
        unto the green.
Quiet Conductor,

how like the termite
        I want to enter the house—
the way Mama Annie

will latch her screen door shut
        whenever anyone steps out
into the heat—for just a minute—

Great Burglar, Lover
        of the Lost,
lend me

your skeleton key
        to this house—
& the one after—

Squall

Today the sun rained down
      on us for hours
before rain shone

        .

silver down
      into the already
muddy ground.

Each day a squall
      chases us indoors
& sends the dogs beneath the house

or drydocked cars
      for shelter.
Tomorrow the mutts will devour

my grandmother's birthday flowers—
      for now, under
thunder they cower.

My young son's excited
      by every boom—
says *Wow* & claps along

as we watch the monsoon
      from Mama Annie's
tiny, tidy rooms.

We fill & flood over—
      without thought, we draw
closer, like the river.

All morning light drowns
          our hatless heads
till at noon rain dances down

& we try to beat it
          out of town.
Pack the car

& gun it to outstrip
          the storm now all
around—the radio

struck silent
          & our son. Right
after we pass

a pickup with mattresses—
          not lying down or tied
but raised upright, paired

in prayer—the beds begin
          to applaud, to clap
together then fly

into the road
          now in rearview.
Headlights following

those just ahead,
          we nose forward
like fog-bound ships,

the lighthouse out—
          wrapped in white
shrouds of rain.

Speed Trap

Stray couch wounded
beside the road
Butts-n-Ribs
Next Exit
100% Virgin Hair
CAJUN FLAME
RESISTANT GARMENTS
Supercool Fashions
Mens Wear
225-925-0000
Dad's Emissions
"Empowering a Chosen
Generation"
The Table Is
Bread
WE BUY GOLD
Soul Food Seafood
Stock Yard Café
"HOT"
BOUDIN
IVY PRIDE TAMALES
Candlelight Dancing Girls
Armadillos, poor
pilgrims, splayed
along the ditch—
Leroy Bar
Best Burger
FALSE RIVER
Washing machine
in the yard
WIN $5000
A WEEK
"FOREVER"

Sodapalooza
Is Back!
Welcome to Port
Baree Speed Trap
sprayed on FEMA trailers
piled like empty
cartons of cigarettes—
No shoes No shirt
No sagging
Best Buy Caskets
Please, Do Not
Flush Any Paper
Down Toilet
LAKE END
The television on
my uncle's porch
loudtalking no one
REVIVAL NIGHTLY
The wind the empty
rocking chair rocks in—
WINGS 40¢ EACH.

Mason Jar

Most miracles
       be small—
lightning bugs

flicking off
       & on
in the dusk before

the storm, hoping
       to be caught
by fire

& each other.
       Instead, children
capture them winking

in jars once
       filled with pennies
or peaches put away

for winter, this waning light
       they drown in
without the air

they are
       meant for.
In this heat

little keeps—
       see how your hat
wilts, held

over your heart to honor
today the dead
who cannot say, yet still

share your name.

Evensong

What music
       the dark makes.
The evensong

of frogs like monks
       in the dusk
making the cedars

their abbey, us
       not their god
but believers who cannot read

yet still see, in the stained
       light around them,
the story of how

we came to be.
       In the alligator's
grimace you can see

who we be
       no longer—
the shark's stomach

tells us where
       she's been
& when—the bezoars, the endless

sets of teeth like gravestones
       that tumble out
& get replaced

by more. Stare
        at the effaced graves—
this gaping grin

of the earth, mounds
        once a wound
in the ground now

almost healed—
        or, earth red
as the gills

of a fish, flaring,
        yanked from the deep
after long struggle—

begging to breathe.

Dog Star

Take today. I want there
        to be less
of everything—wind

& worry, of leaves
        littering the ground
& love letters, addressee

unknown. Return
        to sender—
this, my quarrel

with what
        must be
told. No,

I insist, *No.*

Yet the wind won't
        go away
so easily, the stars remain

& do not grey—
        the boy looking
up into them thinks

he's seeing them first
        tonight—it's true,
here the sky & moon

do meet
        in an overgrown field—
nothing here

tall enough to pretend
to reach—even him
amazed at the blue,

even you.

Balm

Everything
		is everything.
What all

can be
		known.
These are the graves

my dead have sown.
		Each year
they grow, gather

rings like trees
		till I can't count
no more. Beneath their shade

I cast about.
		It is
what it is.

Above, in the blue,
		the moon
cannot be seen

yet shines—
		though really
it casts no light

just mirrors the sun's
		back down among us.
The stones keep me

like bees,
        or a brother. What
balm the weather offers.

Fireflies
        are neither.
All night they try

finding each
        other, lightning
bugs who beacon

& beckon. The mason
        jars we kept them in
as children

are just what
        did them in.
The end

has no end.
        Here the names
of the dead cannot

all be read—
        only understood.
Beneath this stand

of pines, I'll make mine—
        keeping what all
I find. The moon barely

visible in the blue
        of daylight's brine.
Is this where

I'll be buried too?
See you
when I see you.

TRUMPET

Shepherd my tongue

Trumpet

Sink your elbows
        into the sunburnt earth.
Root down

among these mounds the dead
        live beneath,
generations of grass

upon the yawning ground.
        Let cicadas fill my mouth.
Let the crows make of my ears

a nest, filled with every shining thing
        they can find, the names only known
by the fading foil labels

of funeral homes. Knead
        this soil, its brackish bread—
my skin butter the sun

browns but does not burn. I bend
        to the mud, with the few trees
I lean. Shepherd my tongue

with the smallest sounds—
        with the ants
let's descend, fall & file,

our rows irregular as verbs,
        as these graves that grow
without rain.

Let forever the flowers bloom—
        not like the plastic perennials
but these daylilies that repeat

out of the peat, their mouths
        orange & asking,
offering themselves up every year—

sunlight's trumpets, they sound
        their low bugle & beauty
while the sun's flag sinks

& sings. Let the dogs stay
        asleep, silent beneath
my grandmother's house,

wearing black like their mother
        whose paw some stranger's car
ran over, now curled,

broken & unhealed,
        like kin—
she leads them, her children,

through a world that offers up
        only these hours
scrawny & red as the runt

she still loves. The curs call this
        home, crawl under
gutted cars—as if the soil—

to keep cool. Let them eat the heat,
        licking their faces with wind
that calls & will not forget—

what wants to erase
         all the names we hope
to claim. Let this life climb

its ivy over me, let it drag down
         the rust of the roof
of the sharecropper house, the wood

wormed & turned
         to paper, the paper turning
again to leaf—the words—

Let my hands be
         sunk deep
into this dirt that breathes

& breeds these graves, tombs
         like tree stumps
far as you can see.

As near. What we fear
         we find. Everything
but time—

gravestones teeth crooked
         & silver in the gaping mouth
of the ground. These stones hope

to escape the earth,
         wriggling free
like children, impatient—

their ruddy tongues
         stuck out, these graves
taunt but won't

call out our names. At least
           quite yet. My song
my winding sheet.

My bones
           my only home.
Son, when the time comes

cover me in red, rust
           shall be my final bed—
will long outlast

my henna hands.

2008 / 2009 / 2012
May 2014
September 2014
December 2014
January 2015
July 2015
February 2016
May 2016
Summer 2018
Winter 2019
Easter 2019
Quarantine 2020

Acknowledgments

Kenyon Review: "Squall," "Evensong," "Lilies," "Bouquet"
The New Yorker: "Oblivion"
New Republic: "Mason Jar"
Orion: "Egrets"
Paris Review: "Hum," "Shade"
Ploughshares: "High Water," "Dog Tags," "Reprieve"
VQR: "Boneyard," "Dog Star," "Tonsure"
The Yale Review: "Spruce," "Halter"

The poem "Resume" first appeared as a limited-edition broadside for the Beall Poetry Festival at Baylor University.

Kevin Young is the author of fifteen books of poetry and prose, including *Stones,* shortlisted for the T. S. Eliot Prize; *Blue Laws: Selected & Uncollected Poems 1995–2015,* longlisted for the National Book Award; *Book of Hours,* winner of the Lenore Marshall Prize from the Academy of American Poets; *Jelly Roll: a blues,* a finalist for both the National Book Award and the Los Angeles Times Book Prize for Poetry; *Bunk,* a *New York Times* Notable Book, longlisted for the National Book Award, and named on many "best of" lists for 2017; and *The Grey Album,* winner of the Graywolf Press Nonfiction Prize and the PEN Open Book Award, a *New York Times* Notable Book, and a finalist for the National Book Critics Circle Award for criticism. The poetry editor of *The New Yorker,* Young is the editor of nine other volumes, most recently the acclaimed anthology *African American Poetry: 250 Years of Struggle & Song.* He is a member of the American Academy of Arts and Sciences, the American Academy of Arts and Letters, the Society of American Historians, and was named a Chancellor of the Academy of American Poets in 2020. He lives and works in Washington, D.C.

A NOTE ON THE TYPE

The text of this book was set in a typeface named Perpetua, designed by the British artist Eric Gill (1882–1940) and cut by the Monotype Corporation of London in 1928–30. Perpetua is a contemporary letter of original design, without any direct historical antecedents. The shapes of the roman letters basically derive from stonecutting, a form of lettering in which Gill was eminent. The italic is essentially an inclined roman. The general effect of the typeface in reading sizes is one of lightness and grace. The larger display sizes of the type are extremely elegant and form what is probably the most distinguished series of inscriptional letters cut in the present century.

Composed by North Market Street Graphics, Lancaster, Pennsylvania
Printed and bound by Lakeside Book Company, Harrisonburg, Virginia
Designed by Maggie Hinders